HIP-HOP

Biographies

USHER

SADDLEBACK
PUBLISHING

HIP-HOP Biographies

Chris Brown

Drake

50 Cent

Jay-Z

Nicki Minaj

Pitbull

Rihanna

Usher

Lil Wayne

Kanye West

SADDLEBACK
PUBLISHING
www.sdlback.com

ISBN-13: 978-162250-009-3
ISBN-10: 1-62250-009-1
eBook: 978-1-61247-690-2

Printed in Guangzhou, China
NOR/0413/CA21300571
17 16 15 14 13 2 3 4 5 6

Table of Contents

Timeline

1978: Usher is born on October 14.

1991: Usher wins *Star Search*.

1992: Usher signs his first record contract.

1994: Usher releases his first album, *Usher*.

1997: Usher graduates from high school.

He releases his second album, *My Way*.

Usher appears on a television show, *Moesha*.

1998: Usher is the top-selling male pop artist of the year.

1999: Usher appears in two movies and two TV shows.

2002: Usher wins many awards, including a Nickelodeon Kids' Choice Award for Favorite Male Singer.

2004: Usher appears on the cover of *Rolling Stone* magazine. He performs for the first time on *Saturday Night Live*.

2005: Usher wins three Grammy Awards and is nominated for Album of the Year.

He wins a NAACP Award for Outstanding Male Artist.

Usher sings in a concert to raise money for victims of Hurricane Katrina.

2006: Usher appears on Broadway in the musical *Chicago*.

2007: Usher becomes a father with the birth of his first son.

2008: Usher's second son is born.

2009: Usher sings with Justin Bieber.

Usher performs for the inauguration of President Obama.

2010: Usher wins more awards, including two American Music Awards.

Usher releases his sixth album, *Raymond v. Raymond*.

2012: Usher says he will play boxer Sugar Ray Leonard in a movie.

Usher releases album *Looking 4 Myself*.

Meet Usher!

He performed for presidents. He surprised everyone when he hopped on stage at the Super Bowl. He danced and he sang in front of millions of people. He was an actor on a television *soap opera*. You may have seen him on the big screen too. Who is he? He is Usher.

Usher, whose full name is Usher Terry Raymond IV, is not just a multi-platinum recording artist. (A platinum record has sold at least one million copies. Multi-platinum means many millions were sold.) Usher is a singer, a dancer, and an actor. He is a *composer*. He has written songs for many famous artists. Usher is a proud father. He is also a *mentor*, a person who helps or teaches people. He works hard as an *activist*. He does good things for others.

Usher is very popular. Excited fans snapped up over 20 million copies of Usher's biggest-selling album. And Usher has won many awards: six awards from BET (Black Entertainment Television), seven Grammy Awards, and seventeen *Billboard* Music Awards. In fact, Usher was only the third artist in history to have three *singles* in the "Hot 100" list at the same time. The only other two artists to do that before him were the Beatles and the Bee Gees.

Usher was not always a big star. How did he get his start? When did he start singing, dancing, and acting? Usher was like many young people who had a dream of becoming famous. But unlike many young people, Usher *strived* to make his dreams come true. Usher once said, "Strivers achieve what dreamers believe." Usher has worked hard to succeed.

Usher is a singer, an actor, and a dancer.

Usher Raymond IV was born on October 14, 1978. His parents, Usher Raymond III and Jonetta Patton, lived in Dallas, Texas. Usher Raymond III left the family when his son was only a year old. After his father left, Usher's mother, Jonetta, moved the family to Chattanooga, Tennessee. She remarried, so Usher had a stepfather. Later, Usher's mother had another child. James Lackey is Usher's half brother.

In Chattanooga, Usher started to follow his passion, singing. At his mother's urging, he joined the church youth choir when he was nine years old. The choir sang gospel music. Usher loved the strong rhythms and the powerful words. Singing in the choir got Usher thinking more and more about music.

He later said in an interview that singing in church fueled his desire to excel. Usher remembered, "Like any other normal child, I had a lot of dreams."

Usher had the talents he needed to make his dreams become real. When Usher's grandmother listened carefully to the choir, she was one of the first people to notice. Usher really could sing.

Usher started singing in a church choir like this one.

Usher loved singing in the choir at church, but he was singing only for church members and family. It was time to reach more people. Talent shows were a great way for Usher to share his passion for singing. So was joining a band.

When he was eleven years old, Usher became part of a group called "Happy Clowns." The young men in the group were skilled singers and acrobats. But not too many people wanted to see a group that combined singing and stunts. Usher's group decided to become a singing and dancing group instead. The group used the sound and the dance moves that were made popular in Motown.

Motown began when a man named Berry Gordy Jr. built a business in a small house in Detroit. He named it "Hitsville USA." There, Berry Gordy Jr. wrote songs and made records with many talented, young African American artists. Artists like Smokey Robinson, Marvin Gaye, Diana Ross, and Michael Jackson all got their start with the Motown record label. Many Motown groups did choreography, or dances that they planned and did in groups.

With the new dance moves and the new sound, Usher's group changed its name to Nu Beginning. They later recorded ten songs and released an album. Years later, Usher performed as Motown artist Marvin Gaye in a television series called "American Dreams." He told Entertainment Weekly, "People will get a chance to see my love for Marvin Gaye." Usher spent a lot of time preparing to play the role by listening to records and watching films of concerts.

Usher loved the music of Motown artist Marvin Gaye.

Usher's family was excited about his talent, and Usher was ready to go to new places. When he was twelve, his family moved to Atlanta. His mother, Jonetta, hoped that he would get more *exposure* in Atlanta than in Tennessee. Would the move pay off? Someone famous needed to notice Usher to get him started in his career.

Arsenio Hall hosted the talent show *Star Search*.

Usher appeared in many talent shows, and local fans loved his music. But it was a television show that gave him his huge break and helped him gain a wider audience. Usher was only thirteen years old when he auditioned for *Star Search*. *Star Search* was a television talent show. Week after week, the competitors fought to stay on top. Usher was on top for four months! He won the competition by singing a song by a famous group, Boyz II Men. The song was called "End of the Road." But it seemed like Usher's career was just taking off.

Usher had fun on *Star Search*. He later remembered, "I was a competitor for four months. I was doing good. No one could beat me."

Star Search fans were not the only people who noticed Usher. A record producer named L.A. Reid noticed Usher too. Usher signed a contract with LaFace Records, the company where Reid worked. Reid told *Billboard* magazine that Usher was going to be a big star, following in the footsteps of other rhythm and blues artists like Marvin Gaye and Smokey Robinson. Reid said, "Usher represents the next generation of R&B soul." Would his prediction come true?

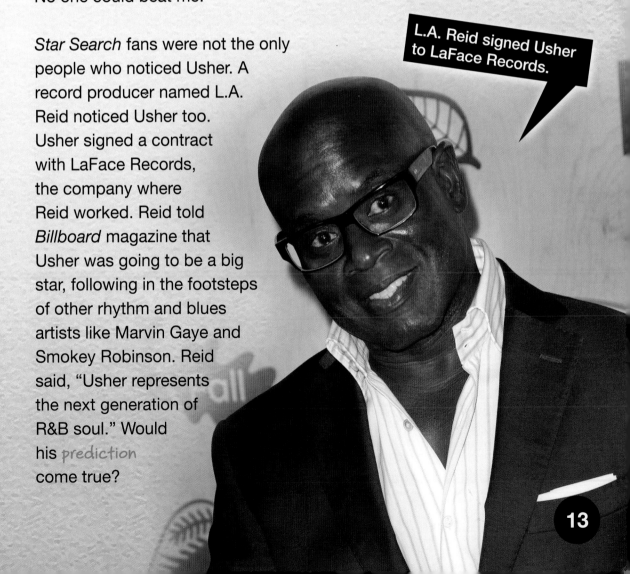

L.A. Reid signed Usher to LaFace Records.

Usher's Early Career

It was time for Usher to get to work on his first solo album. The people at LaFace Records decided that Usher needed a mentor to help him record his album. Part of the mentor's job was to help Usher create his image. An image is how fans see an artist. Usher was a choir singer who won talent shows. Now he needed to figure out if he should change. What would make Usher popular with fans and critics?

LaFace decided that Sean "Diddy" Combs would be a good mentor for Usher. Sean Combs, who was known as Puff Daddy until he changed his name to P. Diddy and then to just Diddy, was a record producer. He was responsible for the sale of over 100 million records. With his talent and experience, he could help create a new image for Usher.

On August 30, 1994, the record was ready. LaFace released Usher's album, named *Usher* after the singer. Usher was only fifteen years old. People were confused by Usher's image. A few years before, he had sung in the choir. Now he looked like a "bad boy." The album sold 500,000 copies. His first single was a gold record, and many people learned about Usher. But the album was not considered a big success.

Usher later told a magazine reporter, "It was the wrong direction. That whole bad-boy thing, me frowning for the camera—that wasn't me."

So who was Usher? What would he do next?

Sean "Diddy" Combs was one of Usher's earliest mentors.

Although his first album did not sell as well as he had hoped, Usher was becoming more famous. He was asked to do some projects that helped his fame skyrocket. He recorded a national commercial for Coca-Cola in 1995 and joined some other artists to record "You Will Know." That single was featured in the soundtrack of a new movie, *Jason's Lyric*. He also did a duet with teen pop star Monica.

Usher had moved from Chattanooga to Atlanta to help his career. Now it was time to move again. Usher moved to New York. All of his new projects did not keep him from working on his second album. The second album was released right after Usher graduated from high school.

For this album, Usher wrote or co-wrote many of his own songs. Sean "Diddy" Combs was still working with Usher, but Usher had made another friend, Jermaine Dupri. Dupri was a producer and co-writer for many of the songs on Usher's second album. Usher co-wrote six of the nine songs on the new album, called *My Way*. The album, released in 1997, sold eight million copies. Fans loved singles like "You Make Me Wanna . . ." and "Nice and Slow." After the release of the record, Usher told a newspaper reporter, "The album is done my way in every aspect. I did a lot more on this album because I'm older and have more of an opinion."

Usher had finally reached a wider audience. Not only did the songs on *My Way* rise on the charts for R & B, but they also were on the pop charts. Usher's boyhood dreams were coming true.

Now that Usher was getting popular with fans, they wanted to see him perform. Usher went on tours during which he sang and danced for large audiences. Usher did not always tour alone. He had a spot in a tour with Sean "Diddy" Combs and other singers. It was called the *No Way Out* tour. He appeared with singer Mary J. Blige. When Janet Jackson went on tour, he was her opening act, which meant that he sang for the crowds before Janet came on stage.

Fans wanted another album after the success of *My Way*. Usher released an album with live performances from his tours. The album *Live*, released in 1999, featured many other popular artists, such as L'il Kim, Jagged Edge, and Twista. Usher showed that he could be creative with others. He also showed his creativity as a stage performer. His dance moves thrilled the crowds almost as much as his voice.

Usher became so popular that he had a hard time getting through crowds of fans. At some of his concerts, people dressed up to look like Usher. They went into the throngs of screaming fans to help him escape. The fans would mob the "fake Ushers" so Usher could get away. One of the people in charge of Usher's clothes on tour explained what it was like to be a fake Usher. He said, "When you get one hundred little girls, they don't become touches, they become hits."

Usher went on tour and made an album of his live performances.

19

What would be next for Usher? He had released albums. He had top-selling singles. And Usher had gone on tours where he was mobbed by screaming fans. Now that he had conquered the stage, it was time for Usher to appear in front of new audiences—television audiences.

Brandy Norwood, known to her audiences as simply "Brandy," is a singer who started her career in 1994. She is also an actress who has appeared in many shows, from *Dancing with the Stars* to a Disney version of *Cinderella*. In 1997 Brandy was starring in a hit comedy show called *Moesha*. Usher got a role on the show playing Brandy's boyfriend. Although he was known as a singer, Usher did a great job with the show. He was a natural for comedy!

Audiences noticed what a great job Usher did on *Moesha*—and so did television producers. After his success on *Moesha*, it was not long before he was offered a role on another television show. He appeared on a soap opera called *The Bold and the Beautiful*. Usher did not give up his singing career, but he clearly loved acting. He told *People* magazine, "I've found a new love. My acting is making me want to leave my singing."

Would this be the end of Usher's singing career?

Brandy Norwood starred with Usher in *Moesha*.

It was easy to see that Usher loved acting. In 1998 he debuted in a film. It was a science fiction thriller called *The Faculty*, directed by Robert Rodriguez. Rodriguez was thrilled by Usher's performance. The director told *People* magazine, "He has a natural style. I was impressed." Just a year after his debut in *The Faculty*, Usher appeared in two more films. He was a disc jockey in a teen movie, *She's All That*. Usher appeared in a drama with another singer-turned-actor, Vanessa Williams. The suspenseful drama was called *Light It Up*.

Usher's work in movies was popular with fans, but the movies were not well loved by critics. Usher's music, though, was getting better and better. Not only did fans love it, but the people who gave awards for music loved it too.

At the young age of twenty-two, Usher released another album. The album, called *8701*, sold eight million copies. Usher won Grammy Awards for two songs on the album, "U Remind Me" and "U Don't Have to Call." A newspaper writer once asked him about the award-winning album. Usher said, "This album is really about my life as an artist, as a writer, as a producer, and as a man."

Usher was a hard worker. He once said, "Sleeping is forbidden at the age of twenty-two. It's all work and no play." Where would Usher's hard work take him next?

Usher won a Grammy Award at age twenty-two.

Usher Becomes a Huge Star

Usher was greeted at concerts by thousands of screaming fans. He was recognized on both television and the big screen. But his best-selling album had not even come out yet. Usher was working on an album that would break records.

In March 2004 Usher released *Confessions*. In its first week alone, the album sold nearly 1.1 million copies. Soon, the album had sold 15 million copies around the world. Songs like "Confessions," "Burn," and "Yeah!" could be heard on radios everywhere. Usher received eight Grammy nominations and won two of them. "Yeah!" won an award for collaborating, or working together with another artist. The album won R&B Album of the Year.

Before the album even came out, Usher knew that it would be popular. He told a magazine, "My feeling has always been that *Confessions* would be a landmark album for me. I knew this album was going to be big. I couldn't wait for it to drop. I was like, 'I'm going to get ya'll this time.'"

It was not enough for Usher to win two Grammys for his own album. He sang a duet with singer and songwriter Alicia Keys called "My Boo." Their song won another Grammy, for best R&B Performance by a Duo.

It seemed like the sky was the limit for Usher. Where would his fame take him next?

Usher won Grammy and *Billboard* awards for his music.

Usher had appeared on many stages, singing and dancing for his fans. His style of music made people dance. But many people were surprised when Usher decided to sing and dance on Broadway in a musical. Broadway is an area in New York City where plays and musical shows are put on. Shows like *The Lion King* have been done on Broadway, where there are more than forty theaters.

Usher played Billy Flynn in the musical *Chicago*.

Sales of Broadway tickets in 2011 were over one billion dollars. Performing on Broadway could help a performer reach a new and different kind of audience.

Usher had won five Grammy Awards when he was asked to play the role of Billy Flynn, an attorney in the show *Chicago*. In the role of Billy Flynn, Usher would not only have to sing, he would have to tap dance.

Usher was excited about the new role. He explained, "I have always admired Broadway actors for their showmanship, dedication, and focus that goes into performing live on stage every night. Being on Broadway allows you to connect to audiences in a whole new way that's different from music and movies." Usher's mom, Jonetta Patton, came to see her son sing and dance on stage. She was a proud mom when she said, "I thought his performance was unbelievable. Absolutely incredible. I am so, so, so happy."

Usher played the role night after night for several months. He had to quit when he got sick with strep throat. His throat was so sore, he could

Usher had already performed with many artists, but he moved onto a bigger stage when he was called to work with presidents.

In 2009 Barack Obama made history. He was the first African American to be elected president of the United States. When Obama was elected, he said to the nation, "It is only the chance for us to make that change." Usher agreed with Obama. He told MTV News, "It only starts here. The mission's not over."

To celebrate Obama's inauguration, Usher took part in a concert with many stars, including U2, Beyoncé, and Stevie Wonder. Obama encouraged the artists who performed at the concert. Usher reported, "[Obama] encouraged us to … speak about the victories of life. Music has always been a universal language. And you choose to use it in the way that you feel." Usher and the other artists sang together to show their feelings of hope for their country.

Usher not only performed for Barack Obama, but he also met another former president, Bill Clinton. Clinton started a foundation, or a group of people who were dedicated to protect the environment and make people healthier. Usher believed in these goals, so he joined the foundation too.

Usher said, "My challenge? To give kids a new look on life. I believe all young people have the potential to be tomorrow's leaders. That's why I've been working to help kids find new ways to serve their communities and change their world for the better."

By working with partners like presidents, Usher started to use his talents for more than just making people sing and dance.

Usher performed at Barack Obama's inauguration.

Usher Branches Out

A mentor is someone who advises or trains other people. Diddy was a mentor for Usher when Usher recorded his first album. But Diddy was not the only artist who influenced Usher.

Michael Jackson was a pop star beginning when he was a young boy in the 1970s. In the 1980s, Michael Jackson made songs and music videos that made him even more popular all over the world. As a boy, Usher watched the dance moves of Michael Jackson. He also watched how Michael Jackson lived his life.

After Michael Jackson died, Usher said, "They say if you ever want to be great, you've got to study who the greats studied, so of course, I studied his moves—studied them down to a T." Usher also said, "I consider myself very fortunate to have had the opportunity to share the stage with him, to know him personally, and I am always going to remember him."

Many people who have been mentored become mentors for others. Usher became a mentor for the famous singer Justin Bieber. Justin was a lot like Usher. He won a talent show in Canada when he was thirteen. Justin and his mother posted videos online of Justin's singing to share with his relatives. Justin happened to meet Usher in a parking lot when Justin visited Atlanta. Usher knew right away he wanted to work with him.

Usher mentored Justin Bieber as he started his career.

Usher sang at Michael Jackson's memorial service.

What made Usher want to work with Justin? Usher explained, "I think it was, first and foremost, his charming, winning, timeless attitude. It's as though he had been there before. When I met him, his personality won me over. When he sang, I realized we were dealing with the real thing. His voice just spoke to the type of music I would want to be associated with."

Remembering what it was like to be young and new to the business, Usher took Justin under his wing and helped him record his first album. Justin and Usher continued to stay in touch over the phone and computer. He gave Justin the advice he would give to any artist, "Either be passionate fully about what you do or don't do it at all."

Usher was passionate when he sang at the farewell for Michael Jackson. At the memorial for the "King of Pop," Usher sang a song called "Gone Too Soon." Michael Jackson had written the song in memory of a young boy who died of AIDS-related diseases. It seemed like a good tribute for Michael Jackson.

Jackson inspired Usher. Usher hopes that he can inspire young artists like Justin Bieber—and young people all over the world. Usher wants to work with all kinds of young people, not just singers and dancers. Of course, Usher still had more music to make. And new things to try out in his life.

Usher released more albums, such as *Here I Stand* and *Looking 4 Myself*.

Confessions was Usher's best-selling album. It won so many awards. After that kind of success, it seemed hard to believe that Usher had more music to make. But he was not done thrilling his fans.

After he got married in 2007, Usher released a single called "Love in This Club." The single reached number one, and then Usher released the album *Here I Stand*. He told a magazine reporter that the album told about the "journey of getting married." He said, "Every word on this album is meaningful. I'm saying, 'No matter where I'm at or what I'm doing, you're the person I'm with, so don't have any doubt about it. I stand *here*.'"

Several years later, Usher released another album, *Raymond v. Raymond*. This album was released after he divorced his wife. The album reached the top of the charts. In fact, it bumped off Justin Bieber's album to be number one. Critics noticed that Usher had a very different sound on this album than on previous recordings.

Usher then worked on another album that was released in June 2012. Called *Looking 4 Myself*, the album had a brand-new sound. Usher called the sound "revolutionary pop." It was a sound that Usher invented with another artist, Rico Love.

Usher focused on other businesses too. He started a record label to help up-and-coming artists. Usher even opened his own restaurants.

Usher is part owner of the Cleveland Cavaliers.

Usher did not play sports as a child, but when he grew up, he enjoyed watching sports. He liked sports so much that he actually bought part of a team. In February 2005, Usher invested about nine million dollars to be part owner of a basketball team, the Cleveland Cavaliers.

Usher became part of a group who invested money in the team. When he did, the team's main owner, Dan Gilbert, explained how Usher would help the team. Gilbert said, "We will look for fun and exciting ways to deliver the best fan experience in the NBA . . . Usher is the 'ultimate entertainer' and will be assisting us in this area."

Basketball is not the only sport in which Usher has somehow been involved. During the 2011 Super Bowl, Usher made a surprise appearance. The Black Eyed Peas were the main performers, but Usher came on stage and sang his hit song "OMG." Some fans said that the song was not just one of the best songs of the year. They said that Usher's performance made "OMG" one of the best songs ever.

Usher's Life Today

One of Usher's proudest accomplishments has been fatherhood. Usher is now divorced from his wife. But when he got married, he told a magazine reporter, "[H]aving a child is something that everyone should celebrate." He and his ex-wife, Tameka, had their first son in November 2007. They named him after Usher and Usher's father. The baby was named Usher Raymond V.

Nine months later, Usher and his son appeared on the cover of *Essence* magazine. Perhaps Usher was remembering the heartache of being left by his own dad when he was a baby. Usher said, "Now I represent what he is to become. He's gonna admire me, he's gonna look up to me. He's gonna say … 'I wanna be like my father.'"

Usher also said, "My son completes me. He changes my perspective on what life is, and what matters."

A few months later, Usher and his wife had a second son, Naviyd Ely Raymond.

His own relationship with his children continues to inspire Usher to help other people and try to give them better lives. Usher's New Look Foundation for children is one of the things that Usher does that will help his sons look up to him.

Usher is a loving father to his sons.

39

Usher has made millions of dollars from his records, television shows, and movies. He uses his money and his influence to help others as much as he can. He is especially interested in helping children to make sure they are given the chance to have good lives. Usher once said, "Somebody has to look out for and protect our kids, and I feel blessed to be a blessing to someone else." How does Usher bless others?

Usher founded an organization called New Look. Usher runs camps and conferences that help young people learn leadership skills. Kids from around the world come together to focus on their talent, their education, their careers, and service to others.

New Look also provides training in Atlanta. Kids who live in the same neighborhood where Usher grew up have a chance to learn how to be good public speakers. They learn to help others with their words and actions. Nearly every kid who is part of New Look goes on to graduate from college.

In 2006 New Look started a program called "Our Block." The program helped clean up New Orleans after Hurricane Katrina. Usher teamed up with a store to sell a special line of jewelry. The money they made from selling the jewelry helped them clean up the streets.

Usher played in a basketball game called "Challenge for Children." The event raised $50,000 for charities in Atlanta. He also performed in a concert for hurricane relief. And he was part of a campaign called "Do Something."
Do Something's goal was to get kids to be part of their communities. Usher is a great example of someone who gives back to his community—again and again.

Usher works with children through his New Look Foundation.

Usher appeared in the unusual stage show *Fuerzabruta*.

Usher loves being on stage. He loves dancing for his fans. He loved performing in the musical *Chicago*. In April 2012 Usher debuted music in another new play. Not only did he write music for the play, he danced to it in a unique way.

Imagine that you are in the audience. You hear Usher singing from behind a wall. You see the shadow of a performer running on a treadmill. All of a sudden, he bursts through the wall, which is made of paper. He dances and jumps on the walls, on the stage, and on the floor of the theater—maybe even with YOU. Above your head, other dancers move and splash in a plastic pool full of water.

This is exactly what Usher did for a new play called *Fuerzabruta*. It seems as though Usher just keeps finding new ways to entertain himself—and his audiences.

What Is Next for Usher?

Usher is a young man, but he has lived a very full life. He is a singer, a dancer, an actor, a father, an activist, and a mentor. He considers his children his greatest reason for doing good in the world. He said, "They make me want to get up and live, you know. I have a purpose that's greater than just … amassing wealth and being recognized … This is real, real life now."

Usher works hard to accomplish new things. He keeps busy. He even said, "Down time is not the name of the game." So what is Usher's game?

Usher released a new album, *Looking 4 Myself*, in 2012. It featured the tracks "Climax" and "Scream." Those tracks may win Usher even more fame and awards.

Usher is continuing his work with New Look, the foundation that helps young people. A conference in 2012 trained future leaders.

And Usher has not given up on his acting career. In 2012 he was getting ready to play an incredible role. He was asked to play a boxer, Sugar Ray Leonard, in a movie. He told *Billboard* magazine that his life was like boxing. He explained, "It's all about striving for greatness and offering the best I have. It's no different than a boxer: Standing in front of the person trying to tear his head off, he has to give his all to make it out of that ring."

Usher has always given his all, from a young boy singing in the church choir to a father of two young boys who wants to help others learn and grow. What will be next in this superstar's life?

Usher continues to take on new projects.

Vocabulary

acrobat	(noun)	a performer of gymnastics, such as walking on a tightrope
activist	(noun)	someone who helps a cause, like a charity
audition	(verb)	to try out for something; to perform for a show or an agent
Billboard	(noun)	magazine that covers the music industry, including record and album sales
choreography	(noun)	the steps designed for dancers to perform
composer	(noun)	a person who writes music
contract	(noun)	an agreement between two people, between two companies, or between a person and a company
critic	(noun)	a person who judges
debut	(verb)	to make a first appearance
duo	(noun)	two of something, like two people
excel	(verb)	to do better at something than others do
exposure	(noun)	the fact or state of being seen by others
gold record	(noun)	a record that sells over 500,000 copies
gospel	(noun)	a kind of music that started as a form of church singing in the American South
Grammy Award	(noun)	an award given to the best recording artists every year by The Recording Academy
image	(noun)	an idea of what someone or something is like
inauguration	(noun)	the ceremony putting someone into office
invest	(verb)	to put time, money, or talent into something
mentor	(noun)	a wise or trusted teacher or counselor

NAACP	(noun)	the National Association for the Advancement of Colored People
passion	(noun)	a powerful feeling
pop	(adjective or noun)	generally appealing; a watered-down version of rock and roll
prediction	(noun)	a guess at what might happen in the future
producer	(noun)	a person who raises money to create a song, a stage show, or something similar
R&B	(noun)	rhythm and blues, a type of music with repetitious rhythms and simple melodies
release	(verb)	issue a record for sale or for people to see
singles	(noun)	recordings of one track rather than a whole album
soap opera	(noun)	a show on the radio or television that shows the interconnected lives of many characters
solo	(adjective)	of or relating to something done alone
striver	(noun)	a person who tries hard
stunt	(noun)	a performance that shows skill
throng	(noun)	a huge crowd
urging	(noun)	encouragement to take action
victim	(noun)	someone who suffers because of an injury or accident

Photo Credits